Teresa of Ávila

(also known as Teresa of Jesus)

1515–1582
Born in Ávila, Spain
Feast Day: October 15
Patron saint of people with headaches,
and Spanish Catholic writers

Text by Barbara Yoffie
Illustrated by Jeff Albrecht

Liguori
PUBLICATIONS
A Redemptorist Ministry

Dedication

To my family:
my parents Jim and Peg,
my husband Bill,
our son Sam and daughter-in-law Erin,
and our precious grandchildren
Ben, Lucas, and Andrew

To all the children I have had the privilege
of teaching throughout the years.

Imprimi Potest:
Stephen T. Rehrauer, CSsR, Provincial
Denver Province, The Redemptorists

Imprimatur:
In accordance with CIC 827, permission to publish has been granted on February 5, 2018, by the Most Reverend Mark S. Rivituso, Auxiliary Bishop, Archdiocese of St. Louis. Permission to publish is an indication that nothing contrary to Church teaching is contained in this work. It does not imply any endorsement of the opinions expressed in the publication; nor is any liability assumed by this permission.

Published by Liguori Publications, Liguori, Missouri 63057

To order, visit Liguori.org or call 800-325-9521.

Copyright © 2018 Liguori Publications

p ISBN 978-0-7648-2793-8

Liguori Publications, a nonprofit corporation, is an apostolate of the Redemptorists. To learn more about the Redemptorists, visit Redemptorists.com.

Printed in the United States of America
22 21 20 19 18 / 5 4 3 2 1
First Edition

Dear Parents and Teachers:

Saints and Me! is a series of children's books about saints, with six books apiece in the first four sets. The first set, *Saints of North America*, honors holy men and women who blessed and served the land we call home. The second, *Saints of Christmas*, includes heavenly heroes who inspire us through Advent and Christmas and teach us to love the Infant Jesus. The third, *Saints for Families*, introduces saints who modeled God's love within and for the domestic Church. The fourth, *Saints for Communities,* explores individuals from different times and places who served Jesus through their various roles and professions.

The seven books in the *Saints for Sacraments* series explore eight saints who had great love for the sacraments. John the Baptist baptized Jesus in the Jordan River. Padre Pio helped people make a good confession. Teresa of Ávila was known for her great love of the Eucharist. Philip Neri received the Holy Spirit after praying to God. Louis and Zélie Martin, a married couple, taught their children to serve God and the poor. At an early age, John Vianney wanted to dedicate his life to God as a priest; today he is the patron saint of parish priests. Maximilian Kolbe battled poor health to become a priest and brought God's healing to sick people.

Name the saint who lived in the desert and ate locusts and honey. In this set of books, who was the saint with stigmata? Who began a Carmelite convent dedicated to prayer? Who grew up during the French Revolution? Which saints were the parents of Thérèse of Lisieux? Who volunteered to die in place of a stranger in a prison camp? Find out in the *Saints for Sacraments* set—part of the *Saints and Me!* series—and help children connect to the lives of the saints.

Introduce your children or students to the *Saints and Me!* series as they:

—READ about the lives of the saints and are inspired by their stories.

—PRAY to the saints for their intercession.

—CELEBRATE the saints and relate them to their lives.

saints for
sacraments

John the Baptist
Baptism

Teresa of Ávila
Eucharist

Philip Neri
Confirmation

padre pio
Reconciliation

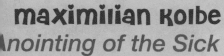

maximilian kolbe
Anointing of the Sick

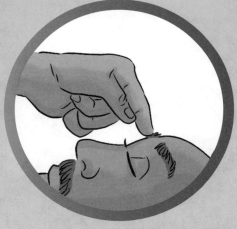

louis and zélie martin
Matrimony

john vianney
Holy Orders

All the saints had a great love for the Eucharist. The Eucharist, or holy Communion, is God's great gift to us. Receiving Jesus in holy Communion helps us grow in holiness. Teresa loved Jesus very much and wanted to be holy like him. She wanted to do great things for the Catholic Church.

Teresa was born centuries ago, in 1515, in Ávila, Spain. She was raised in a large family by loving and holy parents. Young Teresa was cheerful, pretty, and had lots of friends to play with. When she was alone, she liked to pray and read stories about the saints. She thought about their lives and how much they loved God.

When Teresa was in her early teens, her mother died. She loved her mother very much. Teresa prayed to the Blessed Mother. "Dear Mary, I am so sad. Please help me." Teresa prayed to Mary whenever she was afraid or unhappy.

Teresa's father sent her to a convent school led by a group of nuns. She lived at the school with the nuns and other girls her age. She liked the convent school. The nuns taught her many things about the Catholic faith. *"Maybe some day I will be a nun,"* thought Teresa.

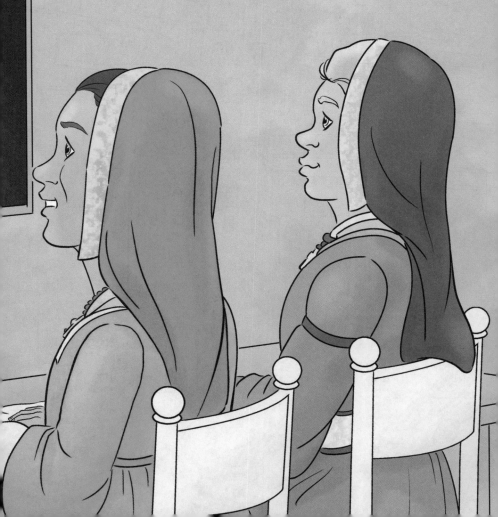

At age twenty, she entered the Carmelite convent in Ávila. Now she was called Teresa of Jesus. Prayer and quiet time were important to Teresa. She also liked to visit the other nuns in the big and busy convent.

Family and friends came to see the nuns almost every day. Sometimes it was just like a party!

There were happy times in the convent
and sad times, too. Teresa was often sick.
Doctors tried to help her. Some days
Teresa didn't feel like praying at all.
But she loved God very much. She knew
God would help her.

Then one day, she saw a statue of Jesus. Jesus was hurt. He looked sad. Teresa thought, *"Jesus, you suffered so much for us. And look at me. I do not love you as much as I should."* She sat down and began to cry.

Teresa did not know what to do. She talked to priests and some of her friends. They told Teresa to pray. Pray when you go to Mass and pray when you are alone. So that is what she did! Praying brought her peace. God answered her prayers and gave her special graces. "Thank you, God, for helping me. Thank you for giving me Jesus in the Eucharist," she whispered.

Teresa knew that Jesus was really present in the Eucharist. At Mass, the bread and wine become the Body and Blood of Jesus. Each time she received Communion, she grew stronger in her faith and friendship with Jesus. She could feel his great love. Thinking about Jesus filled Teresa with joy!

CPSIA information can be obtained
at www.ICGtesting.com
Printed in the USA
FSHW020316061021
85226FS

Teresa loved Jesus and the Church with all her heart. She loved her life in the convent, but deep inside something did not feel right. Something was missing. She wanted more quiet time and more time for prayer. So Teresa made some important changes and started a new Carmelite convent! It was named St. Joseph's Convent.

At first there were problems to work out. "We don't want to change. We like the convent just the way it is! Leave us alone," the nuns grumbled. Some Church leaders questioned her, too. She never gave up because God was with her. It was hard work, but Teresa was a great leader. She knew just what to do. Soon, the changes she made caught on! Teresa was asked to start more convents!

She traveled all over Spain. The nuns were happy living in the new Carmelite convents. The new convents were smaller, with fewer nuns. They wore brown habits and sandals. The Eucharist was at the heart of each convent, helping them to pray and do good works. The nuns prayed for the Church, for sinners, and for people who didn't love God. Life in the convent was simple, prayerful, and holy.

Teresa was asked to write books about her life and her work. She wrote about how to grow close to God in prayer. "Talk to Jesus like you are talking to your best friend. Spend time with him every day. Try to be holy, like Jesus."

Teresa of Avila was a joyful and happy nun who did great things for the Church. She used her gifts to do God's work. The changes Teresa made at the Carmelite convents are still followed today in hundreds of convents around the world. She is remembered for her love of the Eucharist and her important letters and books about prayer and the spiritual life.

Things will change and pass away,
but God is with you every day.

st. teresa of Ávila.

help me to live a holy

and joyful life. like you.

may my heart

be open to Jesus.

Jesus is my friend.

he is all I need to be happy.

Amen.

GLOSSARY (New Words)

Carmelite: A religious order founded in the twelfth century whose nuns dedicate themselves to prayer and sacrifice

Convent: A house where a group of women religious live

Doctor of the Church: A wise teacher whose writings and holiness help the Church

Eucharist: The sacrament in which bread and wine become the Body and Blood of Jesus

Grace: The gift of God's life in us

Holy Communion: The sacrament that makes us one with Jesus, also known as the Eucharist

Mass: Another name for the celebration of the Eucharist

Spiritual life: Growing in love and friendship with God

+++

Saint Teresa of Ávila was declared a doctor of the Church by Pope Paul VI in 1970, the first woman so honored.

Saint Teresa's books are spiritual classics and have inspired millions of people.